HURON COUNTY PUBLIC LIBRARY

S0-CFK-241

HURON COUNTY LIBRARY

Date Due

Hensall	B C 4'77		
Gorrie	Bayfield		
2 Dec 76			
28 Dec 76			
FOR Se91			
Nov 18			
BRFApr92			
F V Oct92			

163824

```
E        Cleaver, Elizabeth, 1939-
j398.2       The miraculous hind; a Hungarian
Cleav    legend.  Pictures and retelling by
         Elizabeth Cleaver.  Toronto, Holt,
         Rinehart and Winston, 1973.
             64 p.  illus., map.


         1. Folklore - Hungary.  I. Title.

                                    26191
                                 A-6209
```

THE MIRACULOUS HIND

A HUNGARIAN LEGEND

HOLT, RINEHART AND WINSTON OF CANADA, LIMITED

TORONTO, MONTREAL

PICTURES AND RETELLING

BY ELIZABETH CLEAVER

163824

OCT 1 5 1975

3

For   Sheila Egoff
Toivo Roht
Judith St. John
William Toye

Copyright© 1973 by Holt, Rinehart and
Winston of Canada, Limited
All Rights Reserved
ISBN 0-03-928278-3
Library of Congress Catalog Card Number
73-6400

It is illegal to reproduce any portion of this
book except by special arrangement with the
publishers. Reproduction of this material
without authorization by any duplication
process whatsoever is a violation of copyright.

Printed in Canada
1 2 3 4 5   77 76 75 74 73

4

Let me tell you a tale of an adventurous hunt for a Miraculous Hind by my people, the Hungarians.

Long, long ago, near the Ural Mountains there lived a king named Menrót and his wife Enéh.

Enéh and Menrót had many children. Two of their sons,
Hunor and Magyar, grew up to be fine and mighty hunters.

7

One day, Hunor and Magyar decided to hold a great hunt, and
began their elaborate preparations.

Both brothers chose fifty of their finest men to accompany them.

The hundred men spent many hours sharpening arrowheads
and spear tips and sabre blades.

10

Even the hunting hounds felt the excitement and grew
restless as they waited for the hunt to begin.

11

Hunor and Magyar chose their finest clothes to wear. They wore fitted jackets, called dolmány, adorned with braiding and beautifully worked jewelled buttons. Over the dolmány they wore sleeved mantles called mente. From their belts and sword chains hung sabres studded with precious stones. On their caps they wore an aigrette.

12

The men wore wide white gathered pantaloons called gatya.
And some had ornate szür mantles.

At dawn, with trumpets sounding and sabres flashing, a
procession of one hundred horsemen set out,

14

and at its head were Hunor and Magyar.

Suddenly a stag and a hind appeared.

Magyar's arrow flashed into the air and pierced the stag's heart. The stag fell to the ground, and a bluebird fluttered high into the sky as it died. But the beautiful wild hind escaped into the forest.

They followed the hind for the rest of that day, and all the next. They crossed a desert and approached a sea, but the hind remained beyond the reach of their arrows.

At sundown they reached the shores of the Kur River, and the hind disappeared. Hunor said, "We shall camp here." Magyar answered, "At daybreak we shall continue the chase."

Planning to find their direction the next day, all the horsemen dismounted and prepared to camp for the night.

In the windy, cool dawn one of the horsemen spotted the hind on the other bank of the river.

Hunor and Magyar and all their hundred horsemen quickly saddled their horses and swam the Kur River to follow the hind.

They crossed desert plains, where there was no grass and not a drop of water to drink.

Then they came to a land where great pools of oil burned and cast a fiery glow in the night sky.

Every evening when the weary horsemen made their camp, they were disappointed and tired of their hunt. But each morning the excitement caught them again with the sense of great adventure. By now they were very far from home, for they had reached the Sea of Azov.

The mysterious hind was often in view, but once, when the hunters approached it, a thick mist descended, hiding everything from sight.

When the sun burst through the mist, the hunters could see once more, but the hind had disappeared.

The horsemen looked everywhere for her tracks in the forest ...

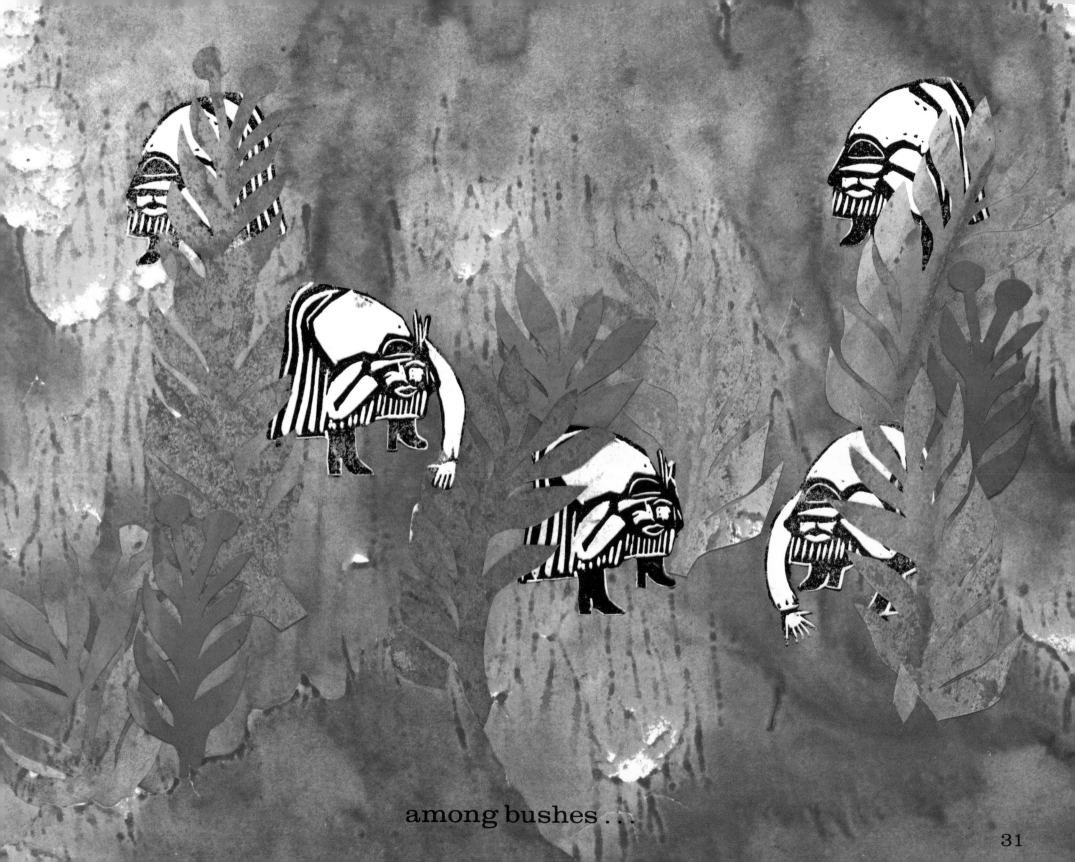

among bushes . . .

in groves of willow trees . . .

and poplars.

Then they realized that they were lost. They had travelled too far.

Magyar asked, "Who knows the way home in this endless world?"

"LET US SETTLE HERE IN THIS LAND TO WHICH THE MIRACULOUS HIND HAS LED US. THE GRASS IS LIKE SILK. THE WATER IS SWEET AND SWEET SAP DRIPS LIKE SYRUP FROM THE TREES. THE BLUE RIVERS HAVE SHINING FISH AND WILD GAME IS PLENTIFUL"

So Hunor and Magyar and their hundred horsemen settled and made camp.

Once rested, they longed for a new adventure and so descended on the plains where the horses were able to gallop freely . . .

and the air smelled sweet with hay, and the scented wind
brushed their faces.

AT TWILIGHT, THE MAGIC TIME BETWEEN DAY AND NIGHT, A STRANGE THING HAPPENED AS IF IN A DREAM - THE MEN BEGAN TO HEAR MUSIC LIKE RIP - PLING WAVES DRIFTING THROUGH THE WOODS STIR - RING DEWDROPS ON THE BLADES OF GRASS.

Quickly the men finished their supper around their camp fires . . .

and rode off to find where the music came from.

They came upon a tent woven from the strands of the mist.
All around it fairy maidens danced and sang.

MANY FAIRY-MAIDENS
LIVED IN THESE WOODS AND
EVERY EVENING THEY ALL
DANCED IN THE MIST.

THE DAUGHTERS OF
KINGS DÚL AND BELAR
ALSO DANCED HERE.

48

The two fairest and prettiest of all were the daughters of King Dúl.

Hunor and Magyar decided they should all choose maidens for themselves. Hunor chose one of King Dúl's fair daughters to be his wife . . .

and Magyar chose the other.

Then each of the hundred horsemen chose a wife.

Together they all rode off into the starry night . . .

TO THE LAND WHERE THE GRASS IS LIKE SILK, THE WATER IS SWEET, AND SWEET SAP DRIPS LIKE SYRUP FROM THE TREES — WHERE THE BLUE RIVER HAS SHINING FISH, AND WILD GAME IS PLENTIFUL

HERE IS WHERE HUNOR AND MAGYAR AND THEIR ONE HUNDRED HORSEMEN AND THEIR WIVES MADE THEIR HOME.   THEIR CHILDREN AND THEIR CHILDREN'S CHILDREN FORMED THE HUNGARIANS.

THE MIRACULOUS HIND
A Hungarian Legend

The legend of the Miraculous Hind is based upon actual historical events that took place on the borders of Europe and Asia some fifteen hundred years ago. It is in many ways an accurate reflection of the movements of the Hungarians through the eastern European steppes between the fifth and eighth centuries A.D.

THE EARLY HISTORY OF THE HUNGARIANS

Fundamentally a Finno-Ugrian linguistic group, the Hungarians are known to have originated somewhere in the region of the Ural Mountains. Around the sixth or fifth century B.C., the proto-Hungarians separated from their Ugrian group, gave up what may formerly have been a forest life of hunting and fishing, and became closely associated with a Turkic tribe or tribes. As a result of this association, they developed into nomadic herdsmen.

Considerably later, in A.D. 463, the Avars left their homeland on the northern border of China and attacked the Sabirs. Pushed westward, the latter in turn attacked the Onogur (Ten Ogurs) people, driving them into the neighbourhood of the Black Sea and the eastern shores of the Sea of Azov. The Onogurs, composed primarily of Turkic groups, included also the Hungarians; thus it was that soon after 463 the Hungarians reached the shores of the Black Sea and settled between the Don and the lower Kuban rivers. Resettlement was relatively unimpeded for shortly before, in 453, the great Hunnish chieftain Attila had died, and his once powerful Empire which had included this region collapsed. The Onogurs mixed with the Huns who had remained in the area; a union which, from the seventh century, resulted in the establishment of Great Bulgaria (Bulgarian means mixed and refers to this union of the Western Huns and the Eastern Ogurs) with which the Hungarians were closely connected.

In 552, the Turks overthrew the reign of the Yüan-Yüans (Asian Avars), who lived in the territory of present-day Mongolia. In a few decades they established an empire extending from the Pacific to the Black Sea. This empire was temporarily overthrown by the Chinese in 630, an event that led one group of the Western Turkish tribes to establish the Khazar Khanat. Khazaria was bordered by the Caucasus Mountains, the Don and Volga rivers, and the Caspian Sea; but its sovereignty soon spread to the neighbouring territories, so that between 641 and 689, the Khazars occupied Great Bulgaria. Before they were overrun, one of the tribes, later known as the Danube Bulgarians, fled westward and established itself in present-day Bulgaria. The tribes which remained, among them the Hungarians, became dependents of the Khazars. Although Turkish society, culture and customs had for centuries influenced the Hungarians, the Khazar Khanat brought even deeper and more lasting changes. Among them were the establishment of dual kingship; the positions of authority, and the names of the dignitaries; the use of Turkish rune writing; contact with Christianity; introduction of agriculture and various trades; and the adoption of various costume elements. The result of this extensive influence led the Byzantines, when writing about the Hungarians in the ninth century, to refer to them as Turks.

About the year 830, the Hungarians broke away from Khazaria in search of greater independence. Other rebelling tribes went with them, among which were a number of Alans of Iranian origin. The new territory to which they went, situated between the Don river, the Carpathian Mountains and the lower Danube river, was called Etelköz (i.e. territory between the rivers). Here in 895-896, as the result of a dispute between the Danube Bulgarians and the Byzantines in which the Hungarians aided victorious Byzantium, the defeated Bulgarians joined the Petchenegs and attacked the Hungarians, pushing them westward into the Carpathian Basin, where they have remained ever since.

URAL
MOUNTAINS

Volga R.

before
463 AD

Don R.

Bulgars

Magyars
after 896

Magyars
830-895

Magyars
463-830

Sea of
Asov

BLACK SEA

CASPIAN

SEA

PERSIAN
EMPIRE

61

THE LEGEND OF THE MIRACULOUS HIND

It is with reference to the foregoing historical background that we return to the legend of the Miraculous Hind. Transmitted orally for centuries, it is first known to appear in written form in a Hungarian chronicle, Gesta Hungarorum, composed in the royal scriptorium by Simon of Kéza between 1282 and 1285. This early text is short, but, with careful interpretation, it describes the history of the early Hungarians. A translation of the original Latin text follows:

". . . Menrót, the giant . . . had gone to the lands of Evilath, in those times a province of Persia; and there he and his wife, Enéh, begot two sons, Hunor and Magyar, from whom the Huns or Hungarians originated. It is said that Menrót had several other wives besides Enéh, from whom he had many more sons and daughters . . . These latter children and their descendants live in the provinces of Persia. . . . Because Hunor and Magyar were the first born, they lived in separate tents from their father.

One day it came to pass that they went on a hunt, and came across a hind on the deserted plains; she ran before them, and led them into the swamps of the Maeotis (Sea of Azov). There she suddenly disappeared before their eyes; they sought her everywhere, but in vain. Hunor and Magyar had ranged throughout the aforesaid swamps and found the lands suitable for animal keeping. So they returned to their father, and with his permission left for good with all their possessions for the swamps of the Maeotis. The Maeotis region lies near Persia; except for an isthmus it is surrounded by the sea, has no rivers, but is rich in grass, trees, fish, birds and wild animals. It is difficult to enter and leave the place. After settling in the swamps of the Maeotis, they did not leave for five years. In the sixth year they went out on to the plains, and came across the wives of Belár's sons, who, in the absence of their husbands, stayed in tents with their children, and celebrated the Feast of the Horn by dancing to music. Hunor and Magyar carried off all the women and children with all their possessions on horseback to the swamps of the Maeotis. It happened that they captured two daughters of Dúl, the Prince of the Alans; one became the wife of Hunor and the other the wife of Magyar. All Huns and Hungarians stem from these women . . ."

Historians believe that this legend contains two quite separate episodes in the westward migration of the Hungarian people. The first, the pursuit of the Hind, represents their move from somewhere near the Urals to the Sea of Azov and the Black Sea in A.D. 463. The second, the abduction of the Alan and Bulgarian women, occurred when the Hungarians came in contact with these peoples at some point after they reached the Sea of Azov (463-C.830).

In 1863, the Hungarian poet János Arany romanticized the legend and included it in his epic poem, Buda Halála (The Death of Buda). It is this poem which every Hungarian schoolchild can recite from memory that has, in turn, served as the inspiration for Elizabeth Cleaver's artistic interpretation. The poem was translated into English as The Legend of the Wondrous Hunt by E. D. Butler of the British Museum (London: Trübner, 1881).

FIGURES OF THE LEGEND

Like the legend, the figures who appear in it are historically meaningful:

ENÉH: mother of Hunor and Magyar. Her name has its origin in the ancient form of the Hungarian word 'ünö' meaning hind. The fact that the progenitrice of the Hungarian nation was called 'hind' derives from the totemistical belief that the nation originated from a holy animal. We find many similar examples in the origin legends of the Central Asian Turks and the Finno-Ugrian peoples, with whom the Hungarians were associated from an early period. Enéh is both the progenitrice of the Hungarians and the Miraculous Hind herself, who traditionally led the nation to their new homeland. The two were separated in the legend by the late chronicler who wished to reconcile pagan beliefs with Christianity.

MENRÓT: father of Hunor and Magyar. He represents the Khazar people, and it is even possible his name is that of a Khazar khagan, who ruled over the Hungarians some time between the mid-seventh and early ninth centuries.

HUNOR AND MAGYAR: brothers, the sons of Enéh and Menrót. Magyar represents the Hungarian people, called Magyar in Hungarian. The name Hunor (not to be confused with the somewhat similar name Hun) stems from Onogur, a people with whom the Hungarians lived for many centuries. The association of the Hungarians and the Onogurs was so close that the Europeans considered them together as Onogurs, hence English 'Hungarians', French 'hongrois', Latin 'hungari', etc. That the medieval chronicler made the association between the Huns and the Hungarians can be explained by the fact that, in the thirteenth century, the Hungarians considered themselves the descendants of Attila's Huns for reasons of dynastic inheritance.

BELÁR: king of the Bulgarians and father of most of the maidens. His name is identical with the word Bulgarian, which both in old Turkish and old Hungarian has a variation without the g sound (i.e. Bular or Belar). He personifies the Bulgarian people. After the defeat of Great Bulgaria in the mid-seventh century, a group of Bulgarians remained in the neighbourhood of the Kuban river. It is most likely that the Hungarians, who lived in the same geographical area, preserved the name of these Bulgarians in their ancient legend.

DÚL: king of the Alans and father of the two maidens chosen as wives by Hunor and Magyar. His name personifies the Alan people. The Alans, an Iranian tribe, lived on the northern side of the Caucasus Mountains from the fourth to the ninth century. Therefore, they were neighbours of the Hungarians that settled in the region of the Kuban river and the Sea of Azov after 463. From the mid-seventh century, they belonged to the Khazar Empire and, in the early ninth century, a group of them joined the Hungarians and accompanied them into the Carpathian Basin.

COSTUMES

The original dress of the Hungarians was similar to the garments worn all over the Eurasian steppes during the first millenium. As only archaeological evidence, particularly in the form of metal and bone objects, has survived from this period, and as historical descriptions are insufficient to enable us to postulate an authentic reconstruction of the ancient Hungarian costume, the figures of the legend are illustrated dressed in costumes now considered typical of traditional Hungarian dress.

The major figures of the story—Enéh, Menrót, Hunor and Magyar, and the daughters of Dúl—wear the dress characteristic of the Hungarian nobility between the sixteenth and eighteenth centuries which survived as Hungarian gala costume until the nineteenth and early twentieth centuries. During this period, the men's costume reflected a good deal of oriental—mainly Ottoman Turkish—influence, characterized by the long-sleeved, fitted jacket called dolmány, lavishly adorned with braiding, embroidery and beautifully worked jewelled buttons. On top of the dolmány, a sleeved mantle called mente was worn over the shoulders. This was usually edged with fur and trimmed with jewelled buttons similar to those of the dolmány. Tightly fitted trousers worn with high boots, and richly decorated oriental arms complemented the dolmány and the mente. A hat adorned with aigrettes completed the ensemble. The women's costumes—wide skirts of rich brocade, fitted bodices with laced fronts, fine long aprons and white blouses with elbow-length puffed sleeves—reflect the mode of the European Renaissance.

The remaining figures in the story—the hundred horsemen, the maidens and the bard—are dressed in Hungarian regional costumes of the nineteenth century. The origin of these peasant costumes can be traced back to the dress of the Hungarian nobility of the Renaissance and Baroque periods. There are, in addition, a few items such as the szür—mantles with large back-collars, characteristically worn over the shoulders with pendant sleeves; and the wide white trousers called gatya—typically nomadic garments, which were undoubtedly brought by the Hungarians from the East.

All of the costumes and their decoration are based upon a detailed study of contemporary representations and of original ethnographic material housed in the Royal Ontario Museum, Toronto. The floral motifs of the maidens' costumes are taken from the recently excavated Turkish tiles that were ordered in 1640 by the Transylvanian Prince, George Rákóczi I, for decorating the walls of the audience chamber in his castle at Sárospatak, Hungary. The same tiles appear as the background in pictures 6, 7 and 8.

Veronika Gervers

Royal Ontario Museum, Toronto

This material was originally prepared to accompany the filmstrip The Miraculous Hind produced by The National Film Board of Canada.